African
Adventures

Dick Anderson

with illustrations by

Dar Dunham

S4632

© copyright 2003 Dick Anderson
Published 2003 by Christian Focus Publications
Reprinted 2004

ISBN 1-85792-8075

Published by
Christian Focus Publications Ltd.
Geanies House, Fearn, Tain, Ross-shire, IV20 1TW, Scotland.

www.christianfocus.com
email: info@christianfocus.com

Cover design by Alister MacInnes
Cover illustration by Graham Kennedy
Other illustrations by Dar Dunham

Printed and Bound in Great Britain by Mackays of Chatham

Contents

The Lost Cow

Keyangak sat on his low camp bed under the African night sky. The stars shone so brightly that he could see his friend Ewoi lying beside him in the sand with his head supported on a little wooden stool and his main garment - an old sheet - tied over one shoulder and thrust aside to bare his chest to the warm air. They had eaten rather a lot of roasted goat meat and washed it down with sweet tea.

Keyangak listened to the sounds of Ewoi cleaning his teeth with a stick from the tooth-brush tree. The scraping noise stopped. Keyangak asked a question

which had puzzled him for a long time. He said, "Ewoi, I want to know how your people came to live in this hot, desert land and why they called themselves by such a strange name. Please tell me."

Ewoi lay quietly for a few moments. "I've heard different stories, and I don't know which is true. But this is the way I think it happened. One evening a young boy - let's call him Esunyun - approached his home just as the stars began to appear. All day he had helped his two older brothers herd his father's cattle. Normally they returned to the village as the sun set, but today they had experienced trouble. They had lost a cow. Esunyun's stomach twitched with fear as he thought of his father's anger. He said to himself, 'Maybe Father will blame me because I'm small and like to play a lot'.

He could dimly see his father seated on his stool as he and his brothers directed the animals into the shelter of a thick wall of thorn branches which protected them from leopards, jackals and even a lion. His mother and sisters moved in among the cows to begin milking. Then he heard his father's angry voice calling, 'You boys come here.' Trembling, Esunyun obeyed.

The old man bellowed at them like a bull, 'A cow is missing. It's White-Eye. Now go and look for her.'

After a drink of warm, fresh milk Esunyun and his brothers set off. The stars shone so brightly that they could just see where the hoofs of the herd had stirred up the sand. But when they arrived at the place where the cows had scattered in search of grass, there was no sign of White-Eye. They built a fire and lay down in the soft sand. Esunyun thought sadly about the lost red cow. He heard a hyena cackle close-by and shuddered as he thought of this fierce creature, like a big dog, hunting stray animals. He knew the fire would keep wild

beasts away from himself and his brothers; but what would protect White-Eye?

At the first glimmer of daylight they started searching for a set of hoof-marks going off alone into the bushes. Quick eyes soon picked up the tracks. They climbed down and down until they reached a sandy plain. Still the tracks led them on.

The sun rose with scorching heat. In the distance tall trees marked a river-bed winding across the dry land. When they reached it they longed for water to quench their thirst but the river-bed was as dry as the desert all around. The tracks marched in a line along the sandy river.

They struggled on until the sun stood high in the sky and their throats ached with dryness. Going round a bend, the hoof-marks suddenly wandered off to the bank, where branches of a tree swept low over the sand. Deep in the shade Esunyun saw a movement. 'Enemies,' he whispered. They halted and raised their spears.

Suddenly a woman laughed. 'You idiots,' she called out in their own language; 'when were young men like you afraid of an old woman? Come here and get something to drink.' Now they saw a small well dug in the sand close to the bank. The old lady came out from the shade with a wooden bowl in her hands. They could tell from the way she dressed that she belonged to their own tribe and they relaxed. Gracefully pulling her goat-skin skirt around her she climbed down into the well and handed them up a drink of clear, cool water.

'Now come with me,' she commanded. She led them through some bushes to a rocky hillside. Passing a small tree they suddenly saw the entrance to a cave. Esunyun ducked to get through the low entrance. Inside, the cave seemed no different from his mother's hut back in the hills. A few kitchen implements made from leather and wood hung from pegs in the rocky walls and a folded cowhide showed where the old lady slept. 'Sit down and drink some milk,' she said.

As they passed the huge mug from hand to hand she told her story. 'I once lived in the hills like you,' she began. 'A great drought struck the land. First our cattle died. Then my family followed until only I remained. I came to this river looking for food. I found plenty of berries on the trees. And here, close to my cave, I can always get water by digging in the sand.' She paused with a naughty smile on her face (because she had already guessed why the youths had come) and added, 'Now see what God brought me last night.' She took them into another cave and there stood White-Eye.

Esunyun flung his arms around the cow's neck and said, 'I thought that milk tasted specially good.'"

Ewoi stopped his tale, plucked his toothbrush from behind his ear where he kept it between meals and started scraping again inside his mouth. Keyangak said nothing, waiting to see if the story might continue.

Sure enough Ewoi replaced the brush and went on, "When they got home their Dad saw White-Eye and his anger faded. A few days later he called all the family heads together. They met under the special Tree of the Elders. Some sat on their wooden stools; others just lolled around on the ground. The really old men spoke first. Everyone listened respectfully even if they had little to say. Then the Father of Esunyun stood up and greeted his fellow elders. 'I want you to hear these lads,' he said. ' They went to seek my lost cow. As well as finding the animal, they also discovered an old woman. I think that lady has a lesson for us.'

After Esunyun's brothers had told their story, Father of Esunyun spoke again: 'We have too many people living here in these hills. God has given us many cows. They can no longer find enough grass. I think we should allow some of our young men to move to the river where my sons found our cow and make their homes in those caves.'"

Ewoi paused. Keyangak heard the tooth brush scrape again. "You know," Ewoi went on; "our word for cave is 'turkana'. Because our fathers dwelt in caves long ago, people call us 'the Cave People - the Turkana.'"

Keyangak lay down beneath a net he had hung over his bed to keep out mosquitos but sleep did not come quickly. He thought of the Lord Jesus who left his home on a dangerous journey, not to rescue a valuable cow but to save people who are much more precious. As he listened to the buzz of the thirsty insects flying around his net a verse came into his mind, "The Son of Man [another name for Jesus] came to look for and to save people who are lost." (Luke 19:10) As he closed his eyes he murmured, "Thank you Lord for finding me. Help me to look for others who feel lost and to bring them to you."

The Mighty Needle

Two Turkana men swaggered up to Keyangak's tent, pitched in the shade of a big thorn tree. They had recently visited the hairdresser who had spent many hours working mud into their hair to produce a smooth pack painted brilliant reds and blues. Each wore a dirty square of cloth knotted over one shoulder and a pair of goatskin sandals. The strings of beads around their necks and waists and a pair of spears in their right hands seemed to say, "Watch out! We are dangerous people." From beneath their solitary piece of clothing each produced a little wooden stool to sit on. Keyangak turned and said, "Hello."

"We bring greetings from Chief Makede. He is sick and wants you to give us medicine to take to him."

Keyangak recognised the name. Makede was the most powerful chief in this tribe numbering hundreds of thousands. He asked, "What is wrong with the Chief?"

One of them pointed to his own stomach and, pretending to be the suffering chief, twisted his face to show great pain. "Sickness eats him here," he replied; "He needs your strongest treatment."

Keyangak rummaged in his box for a bottle of bad-smelling liquid and some tablets. He pointed to the East, where the sun rises. "At dawn give him a teaspoonful with two tablets," he instructed them, "Then when the sun is directly above your heads"...and he pointed upwards... "give him some more. And another dose when the sun is over there." He pointed to the hills in the direction where the sun was going down.

A few days later they returned and announced, "The old man is dead. He says you must come at once." Keyangak knew that the Turkana often make things sound worse than they are. If the chief had really died, he would not be commanding him to go to his home. But he must be seriously ill.

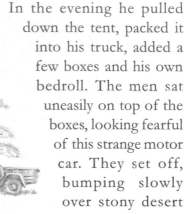

In the evening he pulled down the tent, packed it into his truck, added a few boxes and his own bedroll. The men sat uneasily on top of the boxes, looking fearful of this strange motor car. They set off, bumping slowly over stony desert and sandy river-beds. Just after sunset, the men, pointed to a collection of twenty low huts and said, "That's Makede's home."

Excited children danced up to get a look at the truck. In their midst a dignified elder approached Keyangak. "I am the Chief's son," he said, "Please come with me and I'll show you where he is resting."

The old man lay in the sand using his stool as a pillow. Keyangak noticed white curly hair on the brown skin of his chest. He looked dignified even when sick. Makede rubbed his hand over his belly and said, "The pain is killing me here. Stab me with a needle and make me better."

Keyangak decided to stay at the chief's home so that he could give him an injection every day. Soon the old man was walking again. As he improved he became friendly. Every day he sent Keyangak a wooden jug full of fresh milk as a present. One morning the doctor asked him, "Chief, do you remember how sick you were?"

Makede pinched up the skin of his stomach with his fingers and spread a look of great pain across his wrinkled face. "The pain cut into me here like a spear," he said as he gave his stomach another squeeze; "I knew I was dead."

Keyangak looked sympathetic and said, "Many Turkana are sick. Don't you think it would be good if I could treat them too? I would like to live here so that, when they get ill, I can help them like I helped you." Makede did not reply but he nodded his old head vigorously.

A hundred miles away, across the stony desert, another elderly man lived in a big white house. He ruled the whole district which was half the size of Scotland. When Keyangak had first asked him for permission to work among the Turkana people he had told him, "You travel round for a few months. Camp among the people. Let them see what help you can give them and then we'll ask them to decide if they want you to stay."

At last Doctor Keyangak told this important officer that he was ready to talk again with him about building a school and hospital in the Turkana District. The big man drove from his home in a large lorry full of soldiers, servants and tents. He called all the leaders together. Makede arrived, looking more dignified than ever, and with him four other chiefs and three hundred elders. Many of them had thrust ostrich feathers into their hair, which is their way of dressing up for special occasions.

A servant brought a chair for the proud ruler and the Turkana leaders sat on their little wooden stools in front of him. He stood up to make a speech, but, before he could start, the elders started to hum and then broke into a song about their cattle. Ostrich feathers waved as heads shook in time with the music.

At last the government officer motioned with his hand to quieten them and began to speak. He told them all the good things he had been doing for them and finally talked about Keyangak. He said, "You know this man. He has brought you medicine and wants to live among you so that he can serve you better. I advise you to welcome him."

Just then a man with an angry face got to his feet. He waved his arms as he spoke, "White people are bad. I have seen them in other parts of this country of Kenya. They will take away our land. We don't want them."

Keyangak reminded them that many of them were sick. "You need your own hospital," he told them. "In other parts of Kenya children go to school, but yours are being left behind. They cannot even read and write."

The meeting lasted a long time. Many men spoke. But, when the sun had set and people went away to sleep, the elders still refused.

Keyangak could not sleep. He had come a long way from his own country sure that God wanted him to serve

15

the Turkana. For a long time he walked up and down in the desert wondering what more he could do. He came back to his little tent and lit a lamp. Sitting on his bed he opened his Bible at a place where God said to a man thousands of years ago, "I am the Lord All-Powerful. So don't depend on your own power or strength, but on my Spirit," (Zechariah 4:6).

Keyangak prayed, "Lord, they won't listen to me. You can send your Spirit to change the minds of the chiefs and elders." Then he went to sleep.

When he woke next morning the chiefs and elders had disappeared. The important officer was packing up to leave. Keyangak stayed in his own camp in the shade of a big thorn tree.

In the evening, the five chiefs came to his tent. "Come here and sit down," commanded Makede. He spoke crossly, "You have caused us much trouble. All day I have argued with my elders." Keyangak felt like a small schoolboy, ticked off by his teacher. But the chief went on, "I told them that sickness in my stomach had killed me. Then you plunged your needle many times into my body and I recovered." He paused to chew some tobacco in his mouth and then continued, "We have now decided that you can come and live here."

What made them alter their decision? Keyangak knew only that, when he had felt defeated, he cried to God for help. He chuckled as he thought about his little needle. By prayer God had made it powerful.

Clean Water

The wind beat against a low Turkana hut. A woman, all alone inside the hut, listened to the rain drumming on a cowhide which formed the roof above her head. She looked at her newly-born baby at her side and said softly, "Your name will be Akiru (which means rain) because I cannot remember such storms in all my life."

The storms ceased and the sun shone again as usual. After the rain, pools lay everywhere, making it easy to get water whenever she needed it. Soon the land dried up and Mother of Akiru walked to the river every day. At first she carried her baby in a goatskin tied on her back. But soon Akiru grew big enough to stride along beside her mother carrying her own leather flask, with her skirts made from cowhide flapping around her ankles.

When they reached the well, Mother of Akiru climbed down and scooped water into a bowl. Even though she moved the bowl gently, she usually scooped up a little sand as well as water. Then she lifted the bowl again and again to Akiru who emptied it first into a bucket and then filled her flask. At the end the woman climbed out of the well. She laid a leafy sprig on the water in the bucket to stop it spilling. Kneeling down, she balanced a thick grassy ring on her head and Akiru helped her raise the bucket to perch on the ring. Carefully Mother of Akiru stood up and the two walked home with their day's water supply.

Akiru became sick. She coughed day after day and her body became hot. She felt horrible. Mother of Akiru took her to the tribal doctor. He demanded that she pay him several goats. They did not possess many goats but the mother gladly handed them over for the sake of making Akiru better.

Akiru kept on coughing. She still struggled to the river to help her mother whenever she felt strong enough.

One day, as they approached the line of trees alongside the river, Akiru saw something strange. She stopped in fear and asked her mother, "What's that?"

Mother of Akiru replied, "They call it a motor car. The people from far away travel in them instead of walking like us."

They noticed a group of Turkana sitting under a tree. They went closer. For the first time in her life Akiru saw a white man. She hid behind her mother's skirt, afraid to watch.

Mother of Akiru spotted her cousin and asked him what the white man was doing. He answered, "Oh, that's Keyangak. He's giving medicine to help sick people get better."

As she watched, Mother of Akiru thought of an idea. She would ask Keyangak to cure Akiru.

Akiru screamed. Mother of Akiru called her cousin to help her carry the girl to the doctor. He asked her name and spoke gently to her. Taking her hand he drew her to him and looked at her chest. She cried out in fear when she saw his needle. But she hardly felt it when he plunged it into her leg and injected medicine. He gave her some brown water to drink. Akiru's nose screwed up because the medicine tasted bitter. Keyangak said, "Bring her back tomorrow."

After the sun had risen and set several times she stopped coughing and felt cooler. As strength came back she could go to the river every day. She often spoke to Keyangak and his Turkana friend, Ewoi. And she listened to them as they talked to the elders.

"The chiefs have given us permission to live in this land," Keyangak said to the respected old men, "But where can we find a permanent supply of water? When you bring your sick people here, they will need plenty to drink."

The elders replied, "This river rises in the distant mountains. Water from the mountain rain flows through this dry land of ours for many months each year. Even in the hottest summer, we can always find it by digging in the river-bed."

As the river had been dry for many weeks, they decided to look for water themselves. Ewoi and Keyangak began to dig. Akiru watched the sweat pour off them. They dug and dug until she could only see their heads.

At last Keyangak stopped and said, "Ewoi, we're standing in water. We have dug deep enough."

Keyangak asked the elders, "What is the name of this place?" They reeled off a long name and Ewoi explained its sad meaning, "The Place Where a Giraffe Died Giving Birth to a Baby Giraffe."

Keyangak shook his head. He said, "That does not sound a good name for the hospital we hope to build. We'll just call it 'Lokori - The Place of the Giraffe.'"

They could see clouds over the distant mountains and realised that soon rain would fall in the mountains and fill their river. Friends, who had come from far away to help Keyangak start his home and hospital, built a cement lining to the well and closed it over with a big, steel lid. They placed a pump on the bank to draw water from the well and then thrust it up to the top of Lokori's small hill.

Keyangak stood with Akiru on the rocky knoll when the pump was switched on. They heard a gurgle from deep inside the pipe, then a sort of splutter and finally a whoosh as the beautiful clear liquid poured out and splashed onto the stones. Keyangak cupped his hands and drank some. Then he washed his face in it. He tore off his shirt and splashed water over his body. He collected some for washing his clothes. He was so happy he even danced around.

So much water running everywhere seemed a terrible waste to Akiru. Keyangak called her, "Come over here Akiru. Drink this water. Drink as much as you like. Fill your bucket and take it home."

Akiru looked at the water gushing out of the pipe and replied, "No! I've never seen water as clear as this.

My father never told me that we can get water in this way."

She went back to her well in the river where she had to work so hard to fill her bucket with water that always contained sand. Years later Akiru told her friends, "I was foolish. I liked my little bucket of dirty water more than the clean stream which gushed from the pipe."

One of them answered her, "Eeee Akiru. My life was like your bucket of dirty water. Then someone read the words of Jesus to me, 'Everyone who drinks this water will get thirsty again. But no one who drinks the water I give will ever be thirsty again. The water that I give is like a flowing fountain that gives eternal life,'"(John 4: 13,14).

Keyangak was listening to their chat and joined in, "People are just the same in my own country. All of us are unclean until we come to Jesus and ask him to make us clean. Then he gives us a new life as refreshing as this pure water."

The Hungry Jackal

The red sun dropped behind a range of mountains. Keyangak was glad to see it sink. Many sick people had come to him and Ewoi for help that day and he felt tired. The last patient drank his medicine and set off to walk home. As the fierce heat subsided Keyangak decided to go for a stroll himself. He left the shelter of the trees where he had pitched his tent and wandered out across the cooling desert. He noticed a flock of goats but could not see anyone caring for them. He said to himself, "That's dangerous. A wild animal or a thief could attack them."

While that thought was still in his mind, he saw a fox-like jackal dart out from a bush and run towards the goats. The frightened animals raced away churning up a cloud of sand. But the jackal ran much faster. He sprinted through the middle of the flock, halted and turned to look at them. Seeing their enemy ahead of them now, the goats skidded to a stop. To Keyangak, watching them, they seemed fearful with a sort of questioning look as they wondered how they could escape. They turned and fled in another direction.

The jackal chased after them again, charged through their midst, dashed in front, stopped and eyed them. Once more the terrified animals paused, glanced at their attacker and tried to run away. Suddenly Keyangak

realised what the jackal was doing, "Of course, he's choosing one of the goats to eat for his supper."

He watched the jackal charge through the flock several times. The beast made up his mind. Jumping up, he caught the hind leg of his chosen victim and brought him crashing to the ground.

Keyangak knew the Turkana value goats very much. They drink their milk and eat their meat. They use them instead of money. They get to know each one individually and love him.

The goat bleated loudly as he lay quivering on his side with the jackal's sharp teeth sunk deep into his leg. Filled with pity, Keyangak shouted at the bad beast, "Heh.....You clear off!"

The jackal was a coward. As soon as he realised someone had witnessed his cruel crime, he let go of the goat, looked round at Keyangak and fled to the safety of the bushes.

Keyangak rounded up the animals. Trying to imitate

the herd-boys calling their goats, he clicked his tongue and drove them to the nearest Turkana home. He called the father of the family and told him about the jackal's attack. He asked him, "Please take care of these goats until their owner comes looking for them; for they don't know how to look after themselves."

As he walked back to his camp, some words of Jesus came into his mind, "I am the good shepherd. I know my sheep and they know me," (John 10:14). He remembered some hard times like .... hearing at the age of six that his dad had died, ... being bullied at school, ... later becoming very short of money, ... and, worst of all, feeling pain deep inside himself when he realised what a bad person he had been. He had asked Jesus to become his shepherd and found that, whenever something troubled him, he could cry out to him - like a weak, frightened goat - and his shepherd would set it right.

Keyangak's Donkey

The Turkana were very happy when Keyangak brought his wife and little daughter called Mary to live at Lokori. They immediately gave Mrs Keyangak the name, "Mother of Mary."

Mary often travelled with her dad. She enjoyed sitting on his knee as he drove because she liked to see the road ahead. Her fair hair just tickled him under his chin.

Animals used the narrow, sandy tracks much more than cars. Sometimes the truck frightened a herd of camels and Mary watched them run ahead for many miles before they had the sense to turn off the road into the bushes and let the truck pass. Flocks of goats and sheep used the road too and thought it belonged to them more than any car that came along. Occasionally a Turkana family shuffled along with all their possessions tied to the backs of donkeys.

So many feet on the road kicked up big stones. Whenever rain fell, streams cut ditches across the track. Even though Keyangak drove slowly, the truck bounced around and Mary had to hang on tight. She could hear the thud of loose rocks bashing the metal bottom of the truck and the screech of a thorn tree scraping its side.

She laughed when the Turkana talked about her daddy's truck. They called it his donkey because he always tied his loads onto its back. They said wheels were its legs and lights its eyes. When Keyangak poured petrol into the tank, they exclaimed, "Look, the donkey is drinking!" When the engine made a loud noise going up hill, they said, "Listen, he's snorting!"

One day at Lokori Mary went to look for her daddy

and found him lying on his back underneath the truck. A Turkana told her, "Keyangak's donkey is sick." Mary bent down to look.

Keyangak explained to her that every car has a pipe which carries bad gases from the engine to the back of the car where they can disappear into the air. He pointed to a hole in this pipe and said, "A jagged stone must have hit it very hard." Neither of them noticed a gap in the floor of the cab where the driver sat. The gap was right above the hole in the pipe.

Just then a messenger arrived. "I've come from where the road crosses the river," he said. "A lorry has arrived on the other side. The driver says the river is deep and he cannot drive across. He has supplies for your hospital and wants you to collect them."

Keyangak and and his friend Bill jumped into the truck and asked some men to climb on as well. Mary begged, "Please may I go too?" So she clambered onto her daddy's knee. They reached the river crossing so quickly that no-one smelt gas from the engine swirling through the gap in the floor of the cab.

At the river the men waded across to the lorry. Slowly they brought all the boxes and sacks of supplies to the truck. Only one big box remained. Bill looked at it and said, "That's too heavy for us to carry by hand."

Keyangak thought for a moment. Then he pulled out a big rope from behind the seat of the truck. "Please tie this to the front," he said to Bill. "I'll drive across. If the wheels stick in the mud of the river-bed, you and the men can pull us out."

He turned to Mary and told her, "Sit beside me and hold the seat tightly." Then he started the engine and slowly slid the truck down the bank into the river. It crept across making great waves and, with a loud roar, surged up the other side.

With the big box loaded on, Keyangak started back. This time the truck moved even slower because of the extra weight. Water spread through the gap in the floor of the cab around Keyangak's feet but he did not worry about it as long as the truck kept moving. Out in the middle of the river it stuck in mud. Leaning out of the window Keyangak called the men to get hold of the rope and pull. He made the engine race.

Then he felt Mary's head on his knee. He looked down and received a shock. She had turned bright pink. His eyes went past her and saw the fumes bubbling up through the floor. Immediately he understood and said to himself, "The gas is poisoning her!" As he watched, she stopped breathing.

He thought, "I must get her out of here!" He tried to open the door but the water outside the truck was pressing too strongly against it.

Bill came to the door. Keyangak picked up Mary and thrust her through the window into Bill's arms and shouted, "The fumes are poisoning her!"

Bill realised what had happened to Mary. Standing in the river, with water washing around the top of his legs, he lowered his mouth over Mary's lips and nose. Gently he breathed out and felt Mary's chest expand as air entered her lungs. Then he gasped air into his own lungs and slowly breathed it out again into Mary's.

Fear gripped Keyangak. He wondered, "Will she breathe again? Has she died?" Bill patiently went on drawing in air and blowing it gently into Mary.

Five minutes passed. To Keyangak they seemed like five hours.

Suddenly Mary gasped. Bill withdrew his mouth and Mary started breathing normally. Keyangak cried out with joy and relief.

Back at Lokori, her mother put her to bed. Next day she was running around as if nothing had happened.

A Turkana friend who came to bake bread in Mother of Mary's stove heard the whole story. "Eeee," she said thoughtfully; "Isn't sin like that gas? It leaks from deep inside us and often bubbles slowly up unnoticed .... until it kills. Only Jesus can save us!"

Mother of Mary answered, "God loved the people of this world so much that he gave his only Son, so that everyone who has faith in him will have eternal life and never really die," (John 3:16).

Lion's Food

In Kenya, if you go camping for a few days you tell your friends, "We're going on safari." You will always see plenty of colourful birds and usually some wild animals. So it's exciting and fun. Mary thought safari was a great treat and when her sister, Helen, and brother, Donald, joined the family, they loved it too. One day they set up their small tent under a shady toothbrush tree beside a big river. Many people visited them. While Keyangak saw the sick, Mother of Mary talked to their relatives. Mary was big enough to help her mum cook and keep the place tidy. Helen and

Donald wandered along the river bank until the hot sun chased them into the shade to play.

At last the sun went down and the people walked away to milk their cows and goats at home. Keyangak packed the medicine into boxes and set up beds. His wife would sleep in the tent with two of the children. Their beds filled the tent so Mary said she didn't mind sleeping on the front seat of the car. Keyangak decided to place his own camp cot just outside the tent door. Mother of Mary had cooked some tasty goat stew to warm their tummies.

After supper they asked God to bless the people who had heard about Jesus that day and heal all the sick who had visited them. Finally they said, "Please look after us tonight." They snuggled down into their sleeping

bags and, in a few minutes, fell fast asleep. Only God kept awake to watch over the family.

Keyangak woke early. Soon other people came to the camp. Suddenly a man cried out from the other side of the toothbrush tree, "Keyangak come here quickly."

The doctor walked around the tree. "Look there," the Turkana said and pointed to some marks in the sand.

Keyangak caught his breath as he saw paw marks of a huge cat. "Simba, a lion, was here in the night," he muttered. Helen and Donald came round to look and shuddered as they realised how close the huge cat had come.

"No, no," the man replied, looking at other tracks in the ground; "Not just one lion but three. They smelt your goat cooking last night and came to see if you had left any meat for them. They could not have been very hungry or they would have eaten Keyangak!"

A woman exclaimed, "Oitakoi (which means 'wow')! They've gone off to hide in the bushes but they'll come back tonight. And they'll be hungry by then."

When they finished their work that evening, the family decided to sleep in a safer place. They chose a rocky hill a mile away, where no trees would tempt the lions. Mary slept in the car again. Keyangak and Mother of Mary arranged their low camp beds close together with a mattress on the ground between them. They tucked Helen up with her head at one end of the mattress. Donald slept at the other end.

Mother of Mary woke in the middle of the night. A bright moon shone onto Keyangak's sleeping form and on the children's mattress. She could just see the top of Helen's head on her pillow. But Donald had disappeared.

She cried to Keyangak, "Wake up, wake up; Donald

has gone." Mother of Mary began to cry for her three-year-old boy, "Oh what's happened to him?" Of course she thought of only one thing - simba!

"Let's keep quiet and listen," said Father of Mary. "How could lions walk over all these loose rocks without wakening us?" They strained their ears. Slowly all the sounds of the Turkana night sang their little tunes - sheep bleating in the distance, men talking quietly in a home nearbye, a mosquito buzzing - but nothing suspicious.

Mother of Mary asked anxiously, "Should we go and look for him?"

Just then Helen woke up. Sleepily she enquired, "What's this big thing in my bed?" They pulled back the cover and there was Donald! He said he had felt lonely at his end of the mattress and wanted to cuddle up with his sister.

They all had a good laugh. By this time Mary was awake. She could not help teasing her brother, "The lions must have wanted something more tasty than Donald for their supper!"

Keyangak said, "Let's talk to God about the lions." Then he went on, "Thank you Father that you took care of us when we didn't know we were in danger."

Before his eyes closed, Keyangak heard the quiet grunt of a lion down near the river. "Yes," He thought; "They're hunting tonight; but we're secure up here."

'The Lord is your protector, and he won't go to sleep or let you stumble. The Lord will protect you and keep you safe from all dangers,'" (Psalm 121:3,7).

Hold that Leopard

A man called Ekuwam joined a group sitting around the back of Keyangak's truck. His only piece of clothing was a dirty black sheet, tied in a knot over one shoulder so that the rest covered his body. He stuck his spear into the ground, wrapped his sheet carefully around him, placed a little stool beneath him and sat down. With a finger he removed a wodge of tobacco, the size of a large marble, from his mouth and perched it above an ear so that he could keep it safe and chew it again later.

He looked around. Keyangak was peering into a girl's red eye. Ekuwam watched the doctor straighten up and talk to the child's mother, "When your daughter wakes up in the morning she rubs her eyes, making them a little bit dirty. Then a fly comes along and walks in that dirt. The fly carries disease on his little feet and leaves the germs in the girl's eyes. You should wash her face every morning and then her eyes would not attract flies." Then he found a small tube in a box full of bottles, removed its cap and squeezed a little ointment into the angry-looking eye. "Take this medicine," he said to the mother; "Put some into the eyes every morning and every evening."

He moved to talk to a man whose sore eyes streamed tears. The doctor picked up a piece of cotton wool and carefully wiped them dry. He found another tube of eye medicine in his box and gave it to the man. He advised him, "Clean your eyes every morning and evening and then ask your wife to squeeze a blob of ointment into them."

Under another tree a white woman was talking to

some people. Ekuwam asked a man he recognised, "Who is that?"

The man replied, "Oh that's Keyangak's wife called Mother of Mary. She likes to tell stories."

Ekuwam had not come to hear stories. He wanted help for his sore legs.

The man with the bad eyes moved away and Keyangak turned to Ekuwam. He asked, "Can I help you?"

Ekuwam did not answer. He simply lifted his garment to show his legs to the doctor. From the knees downwards the skin had been torn in many places. Moist blood still lay among clots in the deep cracks. Keyangak gasped and asked, "What happened?"

Ekuwam told him this story.

"My brother and I were caring for our sheep and goats yesterday. Suddenly a leopard jumped out of some bushes. Anger boiled inside me because I love my animals. I waved my stick at the leopard and shouted,

'Kape, tolot!' ('Go away, clear off!'). I hoped to frighten him. But instead he bounded towards me.

What is the use of a little stick against a big, hungry leopard? I threw it away and caught hold of his front paws. His fierce, yellow eyes looked into mine. His hot, foul-smelling breath blew over my face. As I held him up, he scratched at my legs with his hind paws. His claws dug deep into my flesh. He tried to trip me up.

I shouted to my brother, 'Come and help me!'

Fortunately my brother had his spear in his hand. Like a flash of lightening he flung it into the leopard's chest. I felt the huge beast crumple. It fell at my feet - dead. And our sheep and goats were safe."

As Ekuwam finished, he realised that everyone had become silent for the Turkana always love to hear a story of bravery.

Mother of Mary said, "That leopard could have killed you." Then she turned to the people around her, "I too have a story about a brave shepherd who loved his sheep, but this one actually died to save them."

She picked up a little Turkana book and turned over some pages before going on, "A long time ago when I was just a girl in my country I became sad because of the bad things I sometimes said and did. The more I tried to stop doing them, the more I kept on. I felt guilty and weak. Then I read some words of Jesus; just listen, 'Ayong arai ekeyokon loajokon loajalit akiyar kang kotere ngamesekin. [I am the good shepherd and the good shepherd gives up his life for his sheep,]' (John 10:11). I was like a sheep threatened by a fierce animal but Jesus died so that I might be forgiven. He came to life again. I asked him to be my saviour and he gives me the strength I need."

The Dozy Leopard

Keyangak made his first hospital in a small tin hut. A man came to the door. He seemed excited. He spoke in the commanding way the Turkana often use, "Come... and bring your gun."

Keyangak replied, "I have no gun. Anyway I cannot go with you now." He pointed to some sad-faced people sitting on the shady side of the hut and added, "All these people are sick and want my help."

But the man would not give up. "You must come," he repeated; "A leopard has killed one of my camels."

The doctor replied, "I am sorry but I can't kill a leopard."

He would not keep quiet, "Listen. Even if you do not possess a gun, you have poison. The leopard has left part of the meat. He will come back to eat it. If we poison the meat, he will die when he comes for his next meal."

He saw that Keyangak was still reluctant so he tried to persuade him, "Itaouse always helped us." "Itaouse" was his way of saying "Whitehouse", a government officer who ruled Turkana from his centre over a hundred miles away. The man became more insistent, "Whenever Itaouse heard that a leopard was killing our animals and threatening people, he gave us medicine, telling us to place a little in some meat and behold ... the beast died!"

Keyangak knew that leopards often rob the people of camels, cattle, sheep and goats. They even kill people. In fact he had once considered keeping some poison for them but was afraid lest someone give it to one of his patients. He opened his box of medicines and ran his eye over the line of bottles until he came to one with the label, "Sleeping Pills. Take one at night." The bottle was still full.

Keyangak thought, "Mmmm......One pill should put a man to sleep for a night. How many would make a leopard sleep for ever?" He unscrewed the top and counted thirty-six pills. "That might be enough."

"Please wait ," he said; "I will see to these sick people and then we will go."

The sun was high in the sky when they set off over the rocky desert. The man strode ahead of the doctor with his spear ready to deal with the wild animal if it appeared. They came to a belt of trees alongside a river. Already great meat-loving vultures circled in the sky. As the men approached they saw that a few of them had started tearing at a large carcass lying on the ground.

The Turkana man shouted "shoo!". When they were slow to leave, he threw stones at them. Lazily they spread their big wings and rose to join their friends in the air.

Keyangak took the Turkana spear and cut a deep hole in the meat. He unscrewed his bottle and poured in half of the pills.

He said to the man, "Turn it over." Then he did the same on the other side.

Next day the Turkana man came to the hospital. He told Keyangak, "The meat has gone." Keyangak replied, "Probably the vultures ate it all." But the man said, "No. I saw fresh paw marks of a leopard this morning."

Two days passed and Keyangak felt sure the leopard had escaped.

A boy drove his flock of goats to the river for a drink. Suddenly he stopped very still. He saw a leopard. He

clutched his short spear, wondering if he would be able to kill it if it attacked his goats. As he watched it, he smiled. The big animal swayed on his legs and leant against a tree. His eyes were almost closed. He seemed helpless.

He walked right up to the animal and thrust his spear into his heart.

Keyangak heard the story and said to Mary, "I don't like leopards even though they look beautiful and have soft coats. They are cruel, cunning and strong. They remind me of our enemy, the devil who wants to spoil our lives and all we try to do for God. Whenever I feel him at work I say to myself, "Let the mighty strength of the Lord make you strong. Put on all the armour that God gives, so you can defend yourself against all the devil's tricks,' (Ephesians 6:10,11). And then he seems to get weak like that dozy old leopard."

Two Blind Snakes

Many people came to the hospital. The tin hut was much too small. While Keyangak continued to care for the sick people, his friends built a better hospital.

A little girl called Arupe lived two hundred and fifty miles from Lokori. On safari Keyangak found her suffering from a huge swelling of her tummy. He brought her all the way to the hospital where she slowly got better.

While she was waiting for Keyangak to take her home she lived in a tiny house near the hospital with another girl. Keyangak often looked at her and sighed because he knew that, like the rest of us until we receive Jesus, her heart was not right.

The house had no windows, just empty

spaces to let air in. The builders said that when they could find the time they would put in proper windows.

When rain came, Keyangak looked for two corrugated iron sheets (used for making roofs) and stood them on end to cover the window spaces. The girls liked them and asked if they could keep them until the proper windows were ready.

One morning Keyangak and Mother of Mary were eating their breakfast. They saw Arupe rush up to their door looking excited and afraid.

She gasped, "Come quickly. We've seen a snake in our house."

Keyangak left his breakfast. He found a stick and walked off with Arupe. He felt the heat of the strong morning sun soaking into his back. As he approached Arupe's house he saw its fierce light striking the two iron sheets over the window openings. The light bounced back into his eyes so brightly that he had to turn his head away.

When they reached Arupe's front door, Keyangak asked, "Where is the snake?"

She pointed to the foot of an iron sheet. Between the metal and the wall Keyanagak saw a dark space. Arupe hid behind the doctor and said "It went in there,"

Keyangak bent down and peered in, but saw only a gap with no light in it at all. He too was afraid of snakes, even when he could see them. He feared this one much more because it was hidden in the darkness.

He stepped back and took a deep breath. Thrusting his stick under the top of the iron sheet, he flipped it back so that it fell with a clatter onto the stony ground.

Immediately brilliant sunshine flooded into the snakes' hiding place. He saw two deadly vipers.

The snakes lifted up their heads and hissed so angrily

that Keyangak almost dropped his stick. They turned their heads from side to side looking for their enemy. Then he realised they could not see. The bright sunlight, pouring into their dark den, had blinded them. He laughed. Quickly he brought his stick crashing down onto their heads. They rolled over dead.

He looked down at the place where the vipers had made their home and saw only sand and rock sparkling in the brilliant glare. No darkness now; no danger; no more snakes! As he walked back to his breakfast he thought how much he loved the sunshine. Jesus had said, "I am the light for the world! Follow me and you won't be walking in the dark. You will have the light that gives life," (John 8:12). He prayed, "Lord Jesus please shine your light into Arupe's dark heart to set her free from all sin - just like you did for me."

Bandits

Two nurses came from Britain to work in Lokori Hospital. The Turkana easily learnt the name of Essie, but found the other, Mary Moss, more difficult. They called her "Merimoth" and her British friends said she was a merry moth!

One day a girl from the school ran up to the nurses' house. Breathlessly she blurted, "The bandits are here! They're just across the river."

When they heard the news Merimoth and Essie felt a bit queasy in their stomachs. The raiders from the South were more dangerous than lions, leopards and even snakes. These bandits came from other tribes to steal Turkana cows. If anyone resisted them, they fought with spears and guns. The nurses had seen people with horrible cuts in the hospital. Often old folks and children suffered most for they could not run away. Some died.

Essie began to get things organised and along with the terrified girl she quickly walked to the girls' home and told them, "Gather up your sheets and blankets. We're going to sleep on the roof of Keyangak's house where no bandit can reach us."

As the sun set twenty girls followed Essie to the doctor's house. She led them upstairs to a balcony and from the balcony they climbed a steel ladder and then clambered through a narrow opening onto a flat roof.

Now spread your bedding out," Essie commanded. Then she sent them all down again saying, "Everyone go and collect two rocks, as large as you can carry, and bring them up to the roof." They placed them in a heap beside the gap at the top of the ladder ready to drop onto any bandit foolish enough to try to climb up.

Then they all settled down to sleep.

Later that night, Merimoth was called to the hospital. On her way home she got a terrible fright and came running to Keyangak. She said, "I've just seen a bandit. He's standing beside the wall which surrounds our house. And he's holding a gun!"

Trying not to show that he was a little afraid, Keyangak picked up a large stick and asked her, "Can you show me?"

As quietly as they could they crept across the yard separating the two houses. "There he is," Merimoth whispered, pointing to a shadow standing very still by the wall.

Keyangak shouted, "What do you want here?" But the figure did not answer.

Keyangak approached closer, watching carefully. Then a breath of wind caused it to sway ever so slightly and Keyangak laughed. He shouted to Merimoth, "Just watch me beat your bandit!" And he struck it with his stick so that it fell to the ground. Merimoth's bandit was only a bush!

Back in his own house, Keyangak stood at the bottom of the ladder and asked if the girls were all right. Essie called back, "Yes. Most are already asleep."

They slept well that night without any visitor

Next day Essie went to work in the hospital. While she was talking to some sick people she realised they had stopped listening. She saw they were upset. She wondered, "Have I said something to make them angry?"

One darted away... then another... and soon they had all left her - even the ones she thought were too sick to move.

She went outside and saw everyone running as fast as they could. "What's wrong" she asked a schoolboy as he sped past. "Bandits," he replied breathlessly; "People have seen them on the other side of the river. They are running towards us. We must get away."

She asked herself, "What shall I do? Where can I go?" By now everyone had left the hospital. Essie's home was too close to the river and the bandits might already have crossed. She wondered about sheltering with a friend close by. But she guessed they had already fled.

She went back into the empty hospital and looked around. Her eyes rested on the linen cupboard. "That's it," she said to herself. She took out a few sheets from the bottom shelf and placed them on a table. Then she squeezed in, curling herself up so that she could fit between the wide shelves. She just managed to slip a finger beneath the door and pull it shut. There she sat in the darkness, wondering what would happen.

She repeated some words from the Bible she had learnt many years before, "You Lord are the light that keeps me safe. I am not afraid of anyone. You protect me and I have no fears," (Psalm 27:1). She felt better.

She heard voices and wondered, "Are these the bandits?" Her heart beat so loud that she felt sure they would hear it and find her in the cupboard. Footsteps stopped outside the door and she sweated as she waited for someone to fling it open.

Then there was laughter, followed by talk. She recognised the language. It was Turkana, not the language of the people of the South. Then she realised who was speaking - the girl who had come to call her the previous night.

She strained her ears to pick up the conversation and heard her name, "Where's Sister Essie? We did not see her run away when we all fled."

She opened the door and found the schoolgirl and several nurses chuckling. "So Sister, you folded yourself up like a sheet and hid in the cupboard!" And they laughed until tears rolled down their cheeks. Essie did not think it at all funny!

"Where are they?" she asked, "Where did the bandits go? Did anyone get hurt?"

The girl chuckled again. She said, "Someone raised the alarm when he saw young men running about on the other side of the river and heard them shout like warriors. But they were our own Turkana. They had seen a rabbit and wanted to catch it for their lunch!"

The Thief who said No!

Erege worked in Lokori Hospital. Although he had never gone to school as a child, he could read and write quite well. He was intelligent and quick to learn. A pleasant smile usually brightened his face. But he had one problem - a bad temper. Suddenly his anger would flare up and no-one could control him. At these times he would even hit people. Keyangak told him, "Erege. If you want to help people who are not well, you must be kind and gentle. They don't like it when you hit them. You will frighten them away."

He replied, "Yes doctor, I know that. I'm sorry but I just can't control my anger."

Although he tried hard to be kind, he still failed. People still complained about his temper. At last Keyangak told him, "You must leave this hospital."

Poor Erege went back to his home close to Lokori. Whenever Keyangak met him he looked sad. He stopped going to church. A few weeks later a gunshot rang out close to the river. People became afraid. They asked, "Is that the bandits from the South?" Then they found out that Erege had shot a crocodile. No-one minded that a crocodile had died because crocodiles eat goats and even people, but they feared a gun in the hands of such a fierce man as Erege.

Soon they found out why he had bought a gun. He had joined a group of bandits himself. They often raided the People of the South, stealing their cattle and goats.

One day the bandit chief called his men together. He complained, "The People of the South have often attacked the Turkana. They have killed many of our warriors. We are going out to fight them again. This time we will not just take cattle; we will kill people.

A word circled around inside Erege's head, "Nyiaar." That means, "You must not kill." He had forgotten almost everything he had heard in church but at least he had learnt this one command of God. So he told the chief, "I will not go with you. Killing is bad."

The leader became very angry. He shouted, "If you

refuse to help us this time, we don't want you in our gang ever again."

So all his friends left him.

Sitting at home all alone, he thought about his life. His bad temper had destroyed his work. He had become a thief. His friends were murderers. He said to himself, "I have become an evil man." That thought made him very unhappy.

One day people from the church came to his home. Sitting outside his hut on their little stools, they sang some songs and talked about Jesus. As he listened, tears began to roll down his cheeks.

They comforted him, "Erege, don't cry. Jesus loves you and will forgive you if you trust Him."

So Erege talked to Jesus, "I'm an angry man and a thief. I have done many evil deeds. Please make me clean."

He returned to the church and asked the people there to forgive him too.

Because Jesus and His people had been so kind to him, he wanted to serve others. So, when rain failed to fall and the animals could not find grass in the ground or leaves on the trees and the people could no longer get their usual food of meat and milk, Erege wanted to help them in their hunger. He worked in a camp for poor people, giving them food.

And he told them about the only person who can cure an evil temper - Jesus.

Isn't it amazing that the Turkana are just like people every where? Whether we are big or small, at some time we all know that we have evil in our hearts. Some lose their temper like Erege, others steal, or tell lies, think bad thoughts, disobey parents, envy their friends, speak unkindly. Even if we want to get rid of these sins, we often find that we cannot. But, if we have the strength of Jesus, we can. The Bible says, "If we confess our sins to God, he can always be trusted to forgive us and take our sins away," (1 John 1:9). Any of us can come to God and say, "Dear Father, I am so sorry that I have been bad. Please forgive me and make me clean."

Lost in the Desert

On a Sunday morning the sun climbed up behind mountains far away across the river. Its rays slanted across the sleeping form of Lokori's engineer, Jim, who had set up his camp bed on the cool flat roof of his house. A breeze stirred the net which had kept hungry mosquitos away from him during the night. He awoke and for a few minutes lay there remembering that today he could relax. He enjoyed Sundays at the Place of the Giraffe. He need not think about the work which normally kept him busy - building, car repairs, fixing things in the hospital. Lazily he thrust the net aside and rolled out of his bed. Downstairs he spooned some coffee into a machine and lit the gas under it.

A knock at the door jerked him out of his idle mood. Two dusty men stood there, a Turkana and an American. He invited them in and offered them coffee. From the way they gulped it down he could see they were tired and thirsty.

The American spoke, "My name is Tom. We are part of a small health team who are travelling round Turkana giving injections to prevent certain diseases. But our Landrover broke down last night. We left our friends there and have walked for many hours. Please can you help us?"

"Sure," Jim replied; "I'll help. But first we will go to church. Then we must have lunch before we set out."

Jim had two friends who helped him with his building work. He felt sorry for them because they had left their homes in a distant part of Kenya to come and work in Turkana. So they sometimes felt lonely. When he saw them in church he asked if they would like to join him on his trip. The Turkana guide, who had walked in with Tom, offered to go too so that he could show them the way. But Tom said, "You're tired. You get some rest. I know the way."

The four men started off in the fierce heat of the early afternoon. The wheels of the truck crunched on the dry gravel road.

A few palm trees waved their leaves above some water. But Jim knew that the water contained salt and would only make you more thirsty if you drank it. Anyhow they did not need water. Tom said the Landrover was close. They drove on following a road at the foot of a low line of hills. No one noticed a small track branching off to the left. If the Turkana guide had come with them, he could have shown them two sets of footprints where he and Tom had walked the previous night. But no-one saw the marks in the sand and they sped past the turn. After many miles Jim stopped the truck and asked, "Are we on the right road?"

Tom looked around. "I know that we stopped in some hills. It might be those ones." He pointed to a low range fifteen miles away. Jim turned his truck into a dry river which ran in that direction and they churned on through the sand. Seeing some low huts of a Turkana home on the bank, they went to ask if the Landrover had come that way. But none of the four men in the truck could speak the Turkana language so they drove on.

Night fell and they stopped. They had brought no food nor water. They lay on the gravel feeling hungry and thirsty and began to realise they were lost. One of the men saw lights in the distance and said excitedly, "I can see the lights of home." But they were only stars.

They all woke up in the morning feeling cold and thirsty. "We have water in the front of the engine," said

Jim; "but if we use it the engine will not keep cool and will then not work." Thirst gnawed at their throats so much that he decided to open a tap below the engine and carefully ration out a few sips of rusty water to each man.

Tom looked around. He spoke as he pointed far into the distance, "I think the Landrover is in those hills." Slowly their truck crawled across the desert until they came to a wide river-bed with pools of water standing. Thankfully they filled their stomachs.

They felt fresher as they drove up into the hills. But they could not find a way through and turned back to the river. They followed the stream until they arrived at another Turkana home. A friendly man invited them to stay and gave them some goat meat.

This man spoke the Swahili language which Jim and his companions knew. They asked him, "How far is it to Lokori?"

Their new friend smiled, "If a man was to start walking now, he would spend three nights on the way." Jim groaned as he realised they were at least a hundred miles from home and had no petrol. He wrote a note and asked his Turkana host to send someone to Lokori to let his friends know of his problem. Then they all settled down to wait. At least they had plenty of water.

Keyangak and Mother of Mary had spent the weekend at a church in another direction. They returned to Lokori on Sunday evening to hear the sad story. Tom's Turkana guide agreed to go with Keyangak to rescue the broken Landrover with his friends. They found them quickly, helped repair the truck and brought them back to Lokori. But finding Jim and Tom would not be so easy.

They set out along an old road. After travelling for an hour they reached a wide river bed. Half way across

they found the wheel marks of a truck which had driven down the river recently. Keyangak followed until they saw where the truck had run up to a group of huts on the bank. He asked, "Have you seen four men in a truck?"

"Yes," said an old Turkana, "and one of them had no hair." That was our bald friend, Jim. Then he added, "They could not speak our language. They drove right on down the river." By now darkness was falling and Keyangak decided to go home for the night.

He feared the lost men had no water. Back at Lokori he radioed for an aeroplane to come next day to help in the search. When it arrived, he climbed in while friends in a Landrover arranged to meet him at an airstrip close to where he had last seen the lost truck's wheel tracks.

They flew to the airstrip and landed. Whenever the plane came into these isolated strips, any people around always came running to see who had arrived. Keyangak asked them if they had seen a car. "Oh yes," they replied, "a truck came yesterday and died further up the river."

Jim had heard the plane. Quickly he drove his truck into the middle of the dry river. Stripping pieces of bark from palm trees, he arranged them into the word "HELP" on the roof.

The pilot saw them immediately. Keyangak scribbled a note to say that others would come in a Landrover to help them. The pilot tied a red strip to the piece of paper and then zoomed low over the lost people. He opened a window, letting in a rush of cold air, and dropped the note. Down on the ground Jim and Tom saw the flash of red and ran to pick up the welcome message.

Eventually they all got back to Lokori and shared their stories. Jim said, "Whenever I get lost in the desert again, I will turn round while I still have petrol in my tank. Then I can follow my wheel tracks back."

"Yes Jim," Keyangak answered, "and take a guide who knows the way and can speak to the people."

Erege was standing by listening. "Eeee," he said as something struck his mind; "that story is like my life. Guides were all around me telling me God's way, but I ignored them and chose my own. When I saw that I was lost, I should have turned my life round and looked for the track home to God, but I just kept on - always going further astray. Finally, when I could do nothing for myself, Jesus heard my cry for help and came like the aeroplane to rescue me."

*　　　　　*　　　　　*

"All of us were like sheep that had wandered off. We had each gone our own way, but the Lord gave him [that is, Jesus] the punishment we deserved," (Isaiah 53:6).

A Handy Hanky

Keyangak was driving along a forest road to his friend's home. He could feel the mud clutching at the tyres of his Landrover and the cold air outside seeped into the cab. He was looking forward to eating his supper in front of a roaring wood fire. Tomorrow he would continue his journey to Lokori over a hundred miles away in the hot desert.

He had come to collect petrol because Turkana had no petrol stations. On the back of his truck he could occasionally hear a grating sound as two drums full of the precious fuel rubbed against each other. The engine coughed, gave a little spurt and coughed again. He grumbled to himself, "The petrol in the tank has finished. Now I'll have to get out and run some from a drum into the tank which supplies the engine."

Next time the engine coughed, it stopped completely.
"Never mind," he thought; "I've got loads of petrol in
the drums."

He got out onto the muddy road and listened to the
sounds of the forest. The place hummed with life.
Remembering that leopards went hunting in the evenings
he shuddered. " But I'll be okay with all this petrol on
board," he said to himself.

Climbing onto the back of the truck he unscrewed a
small cap on the top of one of the drums. Petrol fumes
swirled out, making his nose itch and his eyes run.

Then he realised he had a big problem. The mouth of the petrol tank was low down on the side of the vehicle. How could he remove petrol from the big drum and run it into the tank? He tried to lift the drum to see if he could tip some petrol out but the heavy drum refused to move even an inch. He looked everywhere for a small cup or tin which he could use to dip fuel out of the drum to the tank, but he could not find anything. He thought, "If only I had a piece of tubing I could suck petrol out of the drum." But there was no tubing on the truck.

Finally he thought of an idea. Pulling a handkerchief from his pocket, he held it by one corner and carefully lowered it into the petrol. Petrol soaked into it and he lifted it out of the drum. Then he clambered down, taking care not to lose too many drops on the way. He held the handkerchief over the mouth of the empty petrol tank with one hand and gently squeezed it with the other. Petrol dripped in, but it was only a tiny amount.

He climbed back to the full drum and let the handkerchief down to soak up another little load of

petrol. Once more he lowered himself to the ground and held the cloth above the mouth of the tank. With a squeeze, a few drops plopped in. After about ten trips like this he thought he might have enough. He got into the cab and drove the three remaining miles to his friends' home.

Next morning he found a piece of tubing and filled the tank in a few minutes.

He said to Mother of Mary, "What a fool I was yesterday. I had all that petrol on my truck but could only use a few drops. In future I will always carry a piece of tubing."

"Yes," she replied; "Jesus wants to fill us with his own wisdom and strength but most people never find him. Others take very little like your drops of petrol. All the time he has barrels of spiritual fuel to pour into our lives."

She continued, "Your car was thirsty for petrol. Jesus once shouted, 'If you are thirsty, come to me and drink! ... Jesus was talking about the Holy Spirit, who would be given to everyone that had faith in him,'" (John 7:37,39).

The Boy who stole a Duck

Mary puzzled over her problem. She knew many people who loved Jesus. The trouble was they were such fine people that they made her feel uncomfortable. One day, when she was going to bed, her dad asked her if she really wanted to follow the Lord. She replied, "Yes, but I'm not good enough."

Keyangak said to her, "Listen Mary and I'll tell you a story."

Mary loved stories. She snuggled close to her father, resting her head on his leg and settled down to hear what he had to say.

He began, "Two servants worked for a rich man. Fat Omolo cooked his food and nine-year-old Edukon cared for his animals.

Although Edukon liked to think his job important, he really found it very easy. His master only possessed a few chickens and a duck. Edukon grew to love them and gave them all names. As they scratched around for their food, he even talked to them as if they were his friends. Whenever he spotted a dog, he imagined it wanted to take a chicken and shot at it with his catapult.

One day the official called him and said, 'Edukon. I'm going away. You must take special care of the animals.'

'Of course Master,' Edukon replied. 'You know I will let nothing bad happen to them.'

For a few days Edukon's life went on as usual. Then he began to think about the duck. 'How the white feathers shine,' he said to himself. 'And how firm the meat looks! I wonder what it tastes like?'

The more he looked at the duck the hungrier he felt.

At last he decided, 'I must try it. Maybe Master will never notice.'

He chased the duck, but it seemed to know that he wanted to do something bad. So it fled, flapping its wings and squawking loudly. Edukon captured it and carried it to a quiet place behind his little house. He looked around to make sure no-one was watching. Then he killed it.

As he plucked off the feathers and cut the meat into slices to fit into his cooking pot, his mouth watered. He perched the pot on three stones, brought some fire from Omolo's kitchen when the cook wasn't looking and heaped wood beneath the pot. The water sizzled and soon the meat began to cook. How good it smelt!

At last he decided the meat was ready. Mmmm, it tasted wonderful. He had never eaten such good meat in all his life.

After a huge meal he curled up on his mat and fell asleep. He slept for a very long time.

Next day he felt a little guilty. The chickens looked small without the duck waddling in their midst. He began to wonder if stealing the duck had been such a good idea after all.

Suddenly Omolo called, 'Edukon.....
Edukon....Come quickly.' The lad sulked to himself, 'What right has Omolo to call me like that?' Omolo commanded him, 'Edukon. Go and fetch firewood.'

'Huh! That's not my job,' he replied cheekily. 'I have to look after these chickens.'

The cook chuckled. 'Oho. I thought you had to look after chickens AND a duck! What is the news of the duck?'

Fear struck Edukon. Had the dying squawks of the duck reached Omolo's hut? Had the lovely smell of cooking meat wafted into his fat nose? Omolo's next words terrified him, 'If you don't fetch firewood I'll tell Master about the duck.'

Edukon went off to look for wood.

He was hardly out of bed next morning when he heard Omolo shouting, 'Edukon. I need water. Go to the well.' Edukon wanted to rebel but he remembered the duck. He picked up a bucket and ran off to the well.

Every day the cook ordered Edukon to work for him. Poor Edukon felt like a slave.

The rich man arrived home. He noticed at once Omolo's big smiles and Edukon's sad face. He asked himself, 'Why does Edukon work so hard for the cook?'

Edukon's face became sadder and sadder.

At last he plucked up his courage and went to the official. 'Please Master,' he said with his eyes looking at the ground, 'I have to tell you something very bad.'

'What is it?'

Edukon continued, 'I'm so sorry. I killed your duck and ate it.'

The rich man said nothing for a long time. Edukon went on, almost in a whisper, 'You can take my wages every day until you have enough money to buy another duck.'

The master answered, 'Edukon, you did something very bad. At first anger boiled inside me. But I'm glad you came to tell me. Because you did not hide it from me I am going to forgive you. But don't you ever do such a thing again.'

Immediately all the sadness left Edukon. He walked out of the master's house feeling so happy. Omolo called him, 'Edukon. Go and fetch me firewood.'

'No,' he laughed. 'I'm never going to fetch wood for you again.'

The cook threatened him, 'I'll tell Master about the duck.'

Edukon chuckled again, 'That's all right. You just tell him. I've been talking to him about it and he has forgiven me.' When he got back to the chickens he laughed at them and said, 'I love my Master very much and I'll never be Omolo's slave again.'"

Mary lay quietly for such a long time that her dad thought she had fallen asleep. But then she asked, "Do you mean that even a person as bad as Edukon can love Jesus?"

"Yes, of course," Keyangak replied; "all of us who want to follow him must start just like Edukon. We listen to that little voice inside us which makes us feel guilty when we sin. Even though we are ashamed, we go to tell him all about it and ask him to forgive us and set us free. Let me read you what he says."

He got up and found Mary's Bible and turned to Isaiah 55:6,7,

> *"Turn to the Lord! He can still be found.*
> *Call out to God! He is near.*
> *Give up your crooked ways and your evil thoughts.*
> *Return to the Lord our God.*
> *He will be merciful and forgive your sins."*

Stolen Tomatoes

Peter lived far from Turkana and spoke a different language. He worked in a quarry where he used a hammer and chisel to cut stones out of the ground for men who used them to build houses. With his small wage he cared for his wife and baby Elija.

Peter was too poor to live in a stone building himself. Mud walls formed his house and thick grass covered the roof. As a boy he had spent only two years at school. Although he could not read and write well, he was good at other things - like shooting.

One day he saw a snake's head peeping through the grass of the roof above him. He picked up his bow and fixed a sharp arrow into its string. Lying on his back, he took careful aim at the beady eye above him and let go. The arrow whirred through the air and Peter heard a squirming sound and then a dead snake fell at his feet.

Peter's friend was a gardener who grew vegetables for a rich man. When Peter visited him one day, he said, "I love tomatoes. Please give me some from your garden." But his friend replied, "These tomatoes belong to my boss." This made Peter want them even more. "Oh give me some," he begged; "Your boss will never know." He persuaded his friend.

Walking home along a winding path, he clutched the bag of tomatoes in his hands. As he drew near he recognised a man waiting outside his house. Peter thought, "Oh dear. I know that man. He's a good man. What will he think about these stolen tomatoes?" He quickly threw the bag into the bushes and hoped his visitor had not noticed. But someone else had seen everything! Who do you think it was?

That night Peter could not sleep. He hated being a thief. He remembered other bad things which he had said and done. He shed some tears because he realised God knew everything about him, even if he could hide some of his badness so that other people did not see.

He tossed and turned in his bed but, as he thought about what he had done, he liked himself less and less. At last he got up and knelt beside his bed. He prayed, "Please God forgive me for stealing those tomatoes. Please forgive me for everything bad I have done."

God changed Peter's life. He became kinder to his wife and children. He stopped some of his bad habits. And he never asked his friend to steal another tomato. Instead he became hungry for the true teachings of God. He struggled to read the Bible for himself.

One day he heard a preacher urge people to find out how God wanted them to serve Him. So he asked God, "Do you want me to be a stone cutter all my life?"

He felt God answering him, "No. You are to be a soul cutter!" What a strange thing for God to say! But Peter soon realised what God meant. Just like he often cut stones out of the ground, so that they might be useful, God had cut him away from the evil in his life. Now the Lord wanted to use him in setting others free. So he went away to a special school where he could study the Bible. After three years he became a preacher and went to work among people of his own tribe who had never heard of Jesus. For ten years he urged people to ask God to forgive them and to accept them as His own sons and daughters. When some turned to Jesus, he helped them understand more of God's truth.

Churches spread throughout Peter's tribe. Many preachers trained to look after them. Peter felt sad when he heard of other tribes who also knew nothing about Jesus. He prayed, "Lord it is terrible that so many have never heard about Jesus. Would you like me to go?"

A friend told him about the Turkana. He and his wife asked God, "Is that where you want us to work?" The leaders of his church told him to visit Turkana. He

asked Keyangak to take him and together they travelled through the desert for many days. Peter had never known the sun to shine so fiercely. He had never seen people so poor. Wherever they went Peter preached and people liked his message. He felt a great love for them.

Peter and his wife worked among the Turkana for fifteen years. Many became Christians. He became the main leader of many new churches. Then, once again, Peter heard of another tribe where no-one knew this great message of God. He decided to leave the work in Turkana to others. With his wife he moved to start a difficult work in another country. Then when war broke out, he had to go home.

Even when he was old, Peter visited churches in his own country. He told them, "Jesus left his own home in heaven and came into this world to die for us so that we might become God's children. Because he loves us so much, we should tell other people that he loves them too. He will even send some of us to different countries where the people have not yet heard his good news. He told his followers, "Go to the people of all nations and make them my disciples," (Matthew 28:19).

God Speaks Our Language

Peter and Keyangak sat in a shaded river-bed near a well. A few people formed a ring around them - women sat with their legs stretched out, men perched on little stools and bright-eyed children played in the sand. A boy called Edung wandered by with his father's goats. He often came there because the animals liked to gobble the pods which fell from some big thorn trees. He wondered why everyone was so quiet. As he came to the outside of the group he noticed they were listening to someone talking. At first he could not make out who was speaking. Then, to his surprise, he saw that the voice came from a box on the ground.

The voice whistled and clucked, "Weet, weet weet; tchick, tchick, tchick, tchick" Edung thought, "That's the noise I make when I'm calling my sheep and goats." It started speaking about a sheep which got lost and a kind shepherd who went looking for it and calling it all through the night until he found it. Edung thought, "I've often done that." Then Peter stood up and, opening a big book, read about a lost sheep and a shepherd called Jesus who had great trouble finding it. When at last he picked up the tired animal, he laid it across his shoulders and took it home with great joy. Edung murmured, "That man loves his sheep like I love mine."

For two years no rain fell in Turkana. All the animals belonging to Edung's father died and the family feared they would starve. They heard that thousands of people had moved to a place beside a big lake where they could find plenty of food.

At the camp everyone lined up. Suddenly Edung pointed to one of the men giving out the food and said to his father, "I know that man. He's Peter the preacher." When he reached the front and held out his bowl to be filled, he said to the pastor, "I met you last year when you and Keyangak came to our home with the speaking box."

Peter smiled at him. "It's good to see you again," he said; "Why don't you learn to read? You have no goats now so you can come to our school."

The teacher often read the Bible to the children. When he had learnt to read for himself, Edung came to love this book because he heard God speaking to him as he read it. He came to know Jesus as his own saviour and shepherd.

Soon Edung became the best in the class. Even though his family was very poor, he spent twelve years in school. Then he went on to learn how to become a teacher.

When he came as a young man to teach at Lokori School, Mother of Mary welcomed him. She had started changing the words of the Bible into the Turkana language and needed a Turkana person who could speak English. She asked Edung, "Would you like to help me in this important work?" They began with stories about the life of Jesus.

On Good Friday all the Christians came to church to remember the death of the Lord Jesus. Edung read them the story in their own language. Two days later he stood up with his book and read about Jesus coming back to life. An old man listened and nodded his head saying, "Eeee, so that's what God really says! I never knew he could speak our language."

The work of writing the whole Bible in Turkana took many years. Edung and his wife finished it long after Mother of Mary had left. When part of it was produced as a small book, a man bought a copy. He said, "I can't read, but I'm going home to ask my friend to sit down and read it to me so that I can learn it by heart."

Now the Turkana do not need a tape player to hear God's message in their own language.

*   *   *

"Everything in the Scriptures is God's Word. All of it is useful for teaching and helping people and for correcting them and showing them how to live," (2 Timothy 3:16).

Eaten by a River

Mother of Mary pressed her hand into her stomach and complained, "Oooh, I don't feel well!"

She watched Keyangak's face as he gently moved his hands over the painful area. An anxious look spread across his face before he sighed and said, "You need an operation." He paused wondering if he should do it himself but did not like to operate on his own wife. So he added, "We will have to get you to Nairobi."

Nairobi is Kenya's capital city, where many clever doctors work in excellent hospitals.

Keyangak knew she would be in safe hands there, but he wrestled with another problem: how could he get her to the city? It lay 250 miles away and he knew she could not bear the pain of driving over the very rough road. He thought about his friend Gordon in Nairobi who had often helped him with his plane. But how could he tell Gordon about his need?

He decided to telephone. You might think that would be easy, but Keyangak knew that he would need to drive for many hours to get to the nearest phone in a town.

He made up his mind and told Mother of Mary, "I'll go there tonight and ask Gordon to fly up for you tomorrow."

After four hours driving slowly over the uneven track, he and his Turkana companion, Kabil, came to a river. Normally it was a dry ditch. But recently heavy rain had turned the land into a swamp and the river was a fast torrent. Keyangak took off his shoes and waded across. Water swirled around his waist. "The truck will never get across this flood," he said to Kabil.

Kabil replied, "Truly. This river would eat your truck!"

Just then a Landrover drove up to the other bank and a man got out to look at the river. "Heh!" shouted Keyangak, "where are you trying to go?"

The man yelled back, "I'm a scientist. My camp is a few miles away on your side of the river. Do you think I can cross it."

Keyangak warned him, "If you try, the river will sweep your Landrover away."

Then he had an idea. "Why don't we both wade across. You can take my truck to your camp and I'll drive yours up to the town. Then we can meet here tomorrow at midday."

From then onwards Keyangak's journey was easier. He sped up a steep mountain pass and, soon after midnight, arrived at a post office where he found a telephone. He heard the bell ringing at the other end of the line and prayed, "Please God, may someone answer."

It seemed like ages before he heard a sleepy voice, "Hello." It was Gordon's wife and he heaved a sigh of relief. She was not at all surprised to be roused from her bed at such a late hour. "Gordon is away just now," she said; "but I'm sure he can fly to Lokori tomorrow."

Keyangak and Kabil slept for a few hours, sitting up in the Landrover, and then drove back to the river. The flood was even worse and they were so glad they had not tried to cross in the truck. High overhead he heard the drone of an engine. He exclaimed, "Look Kabil, there's Gordon!" They could just see the sun glinting red on a little plane and knew that Mother of Mary would get safely to the city.

The two men parked the scientist's Landrover and waded across the river to wait for him. Then they continued to Lokori in their own truck.

*   *   *   *

Keyangak arrived home in time to say good-bye to a visitor, Paul. Paul wanted to drive along the same road and enquired if it was safe.

"You'll have no difficulty except at the river," Keyangak replied. "You may need to stay there for a few days while the water goes down."

After that Keyangak waited for news about Mother of Mary. The days passed and he grew anxious, he kept wondering, "Has the operation been a success? Is she all right?"

Two weeks after her departure the plane buzzed overhead. Quickly Keyangak drove to the airstrip hoping to meet Mother of Mary. Instead only Gordon climbed out. His friendly face was so serious that Keyangak was afraid of bad news.

He smiled in answer to Keyangak's question about Mother of Mary, "Oh! She's fine. She will soon be ready to come back." He went on, "We're worried about Paul. He seems to be lost."

Keyangak laughed, "I know where Paul is. He's camped beside the hungry river. Jump in the plane and we can go and see him."

The journey only took a few minutes in the aeroplane. Soon they spotted Paul's truck parked at the river bank. They circled overhead and dropped some food and petrol in case he had run short. In a little note they suggested to Paul that he return to Lokori in his car and then fly out with Gordon.

Keyangak was surprised to notice a green Landrover standing alongside Paul's. He recognised it and asked himself, "That's the scientist's Landrover. How did it cross the river when Paul could not get his truck over?"

When they all met at Lokori a few hours later, Paul

told them the tale of the scientist's Landrover. This is how it went:

"I left you that day and drove to the river easily. When I arrived there in the evening I saw it was so deep that even a person could not wade across on foot. So I camped beside it.

Next morning I was amazed to see that the water had subsided a little and was lapping around a piece of white metal. It turned out to be the top of a Landrover.

I asked some people about it and they said, 'That belongs to a scientist. He wanted to use his Landrover on this side of the river and thought he could drive it across. But the river ate it. He's gone up to the town to look for help.'

I have a chain on the front of my truck and a powerful machine which pulls. I hooked it onto the front of the Landrover and tugged it out. Of course water had washed mud into everything. I had nothing to do but wait for the river to go down. So I took the Landrover to pieces, cleaned all the parts and put it together again. By the time the owner returned with someone to help him, his Landrover was all right."

Paul flew off with Gordon.

The next time Gordon arrived he brought Mother of Mary. Her pain had been cured and she wanted to hear all the news of Lokori. She had a good laugh at Paul's story. Then she thought for a minute and became serious. She said, "That scientist heard your warning

but did not heed it. You told him about the danger of driving into the river but he plunged in. The mud gripped the car's wheels and then the flood drowned it. God kindly gives us his laws to guide us through life but we often ignore them. When we disobey him, we get stuck and then trouble flows over us just like the river ate that Landrover. This time Keyangak had the last word, "Isn't it good that even then Jesus can pull us out and wash us clean inside?"

*   *   *

"Obey God's message! Don't fool yourselves by just listening to it," James 1:22.

Tummy Ache

Someone else cried about a sore tummy. On the day he was born his mummy saw a motor car for the first time in her life, so she named her son, "Amotoka". About ten years later, the boy screwed up his face as he clutched at his stomach and cried out, "Mummy. Pain is eating me here."

Mother of Amotoka told him to lie down in the sand while she had a look.

What she saw made her unhappy. His tummy had swollen. She thought, "Perhaps we can cure Amotoka by making lots of cuts in his skin so that blood will flow out and wash the sickness away."

She asked her sister to hold Amotoka while she made a line of cuts across the swelling. Poor Amotoka screamed. His mother then rubbed black ash from the fire into the wounds.

Those wounds felt very sore for several weeks but Amotoka's tummy just grew bigger and bigger. It became so large that Amotoka could not see his feet when he looked down.

Amotoka's family lived a long walk from some big wells surrounded by trees. Alongside the line of trees people had cleared a strip of desert for Keyangak's bird. Every two months Keyangak flew into this strip. When the plane had landed, he and the pilot carried several boxes under the trees, where they waited for the sick. Usually people did not know when to expect him; so they started walking to his little camp as soon as they heard the plane overhead. As many lived far away, he liked to sleep there to make sure they had enough time to arrive.

Mother of Amotoka listened every day for the plane. One morning she caught the distant throb of the engine. She called Amotoka, "Come quickly. That's the bird of Keyangak. We're going to see if he has medicine to make you better."

But you can't move quickly when your tummy is as big as Amotoka's. Mother of Amotoka began to fear that they would arrive too late. By evening she could see the trees around the well in the distance. As they drew close, she made out the shape of the plane.

She told the boy to sit beside a tree while she went to call Keyangak. When he heard the woman approach Keyangak looked up and greeted her. She replied with one word, "Bua" (which means "come"). Keyangak picked up a lamp and followed her. His heart sank as soon as he saw the big swelling. He told Mother of Amotoka, "I'm sorry I have no medicine to cure this. But sleep here and we'll talk in the morning." He knew what he wanted to do, but he thought Mother of Amotoka might not like it.

And he was right! After they had all slept he went to see her again. "Mother," he addressed her respectfully, "I can only take this disease away with a knife. Your son will need to come with me and I will bring him back in two months. If God helps him, he'll be better by then." He explained how he would give Amotoka some medicine to make him sleep and then carefully cut the swelling out.

"Oitakoi, oitakoi!" cried the woman, (a Turkana word expressing shock). "You mean you want to cut him open like we cut up a dead goat!"

Patiently Keyangak explained that Amotoka would only be asleep, but would not feel anything. At the end he would wake up and find his tummy normal.

She asked, "Will you take him away in the bird?"

85

"You can walk with him if you like," replied Keyangak. "But I live far away. You would sleep fifteen nights on the journey."

Mother of Amotoka knew that her boy was getting worse. Soon he would die if he got no help. He might as well die at Keyangak's home. She sat with him while the doctor saw other sick people. Then she said, "Take him and go!"

Amotoka allowed the pilot to lift him into the small plane. Everything seemed so strange that he just sat in silence, even when the engine roared to life.

After a long time he felt a bump. The noise suddenly stopped and doors opened. Keyangak lifted him out and he looked around. He saw some Turkana boys caring for a flock of goats, but the country did not look like anywhere he knew in Turkana. In the distance, beneath the setting sun, he noticed mountains. He thought, "My home must be over there, on the other side of those hills."

Keyangak took him to a brick building. A lady in white clothes washed him all over and showed him where to sleep. He had never seen a bed before and the sheets on it were so clean! He was afraid of falling off in the night, so, after the lady left, he took one of the sheets outside to a patch of soft sand, wrapped it round his weak, swollen body and slept. Amotoka felt terribly lonely. He wished his mummy had come with him.

In the next few days he talked to others in this strange place. They showed him where the doctor cut people like him. The lady in white came several times to stick a needle into him and remove some of his bright red blood. Everything was so different from home! He became afraid.

Keyangak sat on Amotoka's bed one evening. He said, "Tomorrow we will help you go to sleep and then we will take this disease away. First I will talk to Jesus about it," and he asked someone called Jesus to heal Amotoka.

Amotoka woke just as the stars faded and the first glimmer of daylight appeared. He went to a tap and drank lots of water. Then he folded the sheet, slung it over his shoulder and walked towards the mountains. He did not know that his home was 300 miles away.

The sun had just risen when the nurse came to get Amotoka ready for his operation. She found his bed empty. She asked the man in the next bed, "Where has he gone?"

"Who knows?" The man replied. "He left before I woke up."

Nurses searched the hospital, the school and asked in all the nearby homes. They looked under the trees along the Lokori river. But no-one had seen Amotoka. Keyangak jumped into his truck and set out along the road that went past the mountains. After driving for an hour, he saw a small figure in the distance, walking slowly. Amotoka looked ashamed. And he was very tired. All the way back to the hospital he said nothing.

The morning after his operation, Amotoka woke after a very long sleep. He looked downwards. He could see his feet! His tummy was flat! Of course it was sore, but suddenly it felt so light. His wound healed quickly. Eating good food every day, he became strong. As his strength came back, he ran all round the school and the hospital. Everyone in the small township at Lokori came to know Amotoka. He became a happy boy full of talk and good fun. All loved him.

Many days later, Mother of Amotoka was returning to her home with her few goats in the evening when she heard the throb of the plane. She called her sister to care for the goats and set off to the well immediately. As she walked she said to herself, "Don't be silly! When you let Amotoka go in the big bird, you knew he would never come back."

With a sad heart she walked quickly, arriving after dark. She stood silently under the trees looking into the pool of light made by Keyangak's lamp. Three figures sat around the fire as the soup cooked. She made out two men and a child.

Suddenly she shouted, "Oitakoi! Amotoka has come!"

As she hugged him, Mother of Amotoka could feel that his swelling had completely disappeared. Joy bubbled up in her as she said, "Eeee! I thought my son had died and behold he is alive." Keyangak heard her and said, "I want to tell you a story about a lost son who came home but it can wait

until tomorrow. Drink some soup and find some soft sand where you and Amotoka can sleep."

Next morning he came over to them, sat down in the sand and said, "A boy left his father's home, taking much of his wealth, and arrived at a distant country where he wasted the riches in wild living. Then famine came to that land and the boy became terribly hungry. He decided to go home but thought, 'My father will be angry; I must tell him that I'm sorry I've been so bad.'

When he was still a long way off, his father saw him and felt sorry for him. Running to him he flung his arms around him and kissed him.

The son said, 'Father I have sinned ... I am no longer good enough to be called your son,' (Luke 15:21). But the father was so glad to have him back that he ordered servants to bring some new clothes and prepare a great feast. He said, 'this son of mine was dead but has now come back to life. He was lost but has now been found,' (Luke 15:24).

Just as Amotoka nearly died of a terrible disease, so we all have sin in our hearts. It cuts us off from God our Father and makes us live far away from him. He is waiting for each of us to come home to him and tell him that we are so sorry we have rebelled against him. When we do that, he receives us with joy like you welcomed Amotoka."

The white man in this story is a doctor. When he went to Africa many people came to see him about their chest trouble and they kept hearing him say, "Take a deep breath." So that's the name they gave him - in their language, "Keyangak." Many years later two small girls, called Kate and Miriam, kept pleading with him, "Please Grandad, tell us a story" and then, "Why don't you write them in a book?" Another question they asked was, "Is that story true?" And Keyangak usually answered, "Yes, that actually happened but I have changed it a little to help you understand." He also altered some of the names because he does not wish his friends to feel uncomfortable.

A NOTE ON NAMES. Most names in Turkana have a meaning . "Ewoi" is a thorn tree and "Esunyun" means sand. Probably the first young man was born under a thorn tree and (you've guessed it) the second was born in the sand. Children are so important that people call a man by the name of his child. So the Elders in the story call the angry old man, "Father of Esunyun."

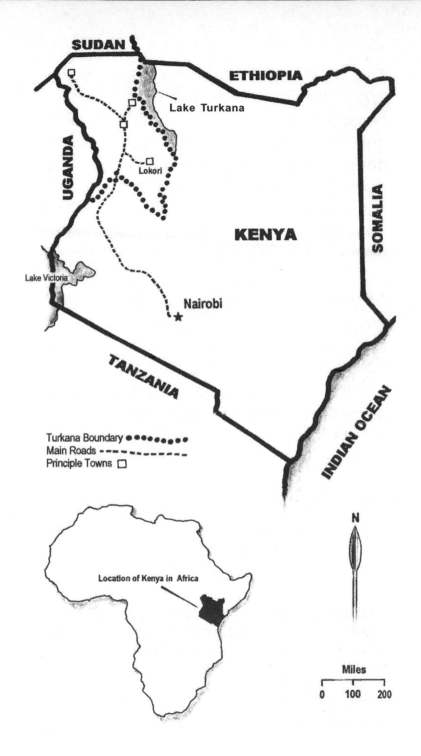

SUDAN

ETHIOPIA

Lake Turkana

UGANDA

Lokori

KENYA

SOMALIA

Lake Victoria

Nairobi
★

TANZANIA

INDIAN OCEAN

Turkana Boundary ●●●●●●●●●●
Main Roads - - - - - - - - - - -
Principle Towns ☐

Location of Kenya in Africa

N

Miles

0   100   200

Rainforest Adventures

The Amazon Rainforest: This is the oldest and largest rainforest in the world. It covers a huge area of South America and has the most varied plant and animal habitat on the planet. When you read this book you will be part of an expedition and adventure into the heart of the rainforest.

Read about the Tree Frog's nest, about the Chameleon who can change colour and the very hungry Piranha fish. Even the Possum can teach a lesson about speaking out for Jesus Christ and the Parasol Ant can show us how to not give up. Then there's the brightly coloured toucan whose call reminds us that with God we can do anything!

Discover what it's like to actually live in the rain forest. Join in the adventures and experience the exciting and dangerous life of a pionerr missionary in South America.

ISBN: 1-85792-627-2

Amazon Adventures

The Amazon Rain Forest: This is the oldest and largest rain forest in the world and one of the longest rivers on the planet cuts through its heart.

It covers a huge area of South America and has the most varied plant and animal habitat on the planet. When you read this book you will be part of an expedition and adventure into its very centre.

Read about the Shocking Electric Eel, the Jungle turncoat, the persistent frog and the mysterious Kinkajou. Find out what lessons we can learn from these wonderful and amazing animals. Even the little white butterflies can teach us something about life and the love of God.

Discover what it's like to actually live in the rain forest. Join in the adventures and experience the exciting and dangerous life of a pioneer missionary in South America.

ISBN: 1-85792-4401

Trailblazers

If you enjoyed this book about real life missionary adventures then you will love these.

Gladys Aylward, No Mountain too High
ISBN 1-85792-594-7
** NEW **

Corrie ten Boom, The Watchmaker's Daughter ISBN
1 85792 116X

Adoniram Judson, Danger on the Streets of Gold
ISBN 1 85792 6609

Isobel Kuhn, Lights in Lisuland
ISBN 1 85792 6102

C.S. Lewis - The Storyteller
ISBN 1 85792 4878

Martyn Lloyd-Jones - From Wales to Westminster
ISBN 1 85792 3499

George Müller; The Children's Champion
ISBN 1 85792 5491

John Newton, A Slave Set Free
NEW
ISBN 1 85792 834 2

John Paton, A South Sea Island Rescue
NEW
ISBN 1 85792 852 0

Mary Slessor, Servant to the Slave
ISBN 1 85792 3480

Joni Eareckson Tada, Swimming against the Tide
NEW
ISBN 1 85792 833 4

Hudson Taylor, An Adventure Begins
ISBN 1 85792 4231

William Wilberforce, The Freedom Fighter
ISBN 1 85792 3715

Richard Wurmbrand, A Voice in the Dark
ISBN 1 85792 2980

CHRISTIAN FOCUS

Staying faithful. Reaching out.

Christian Focus Publications publishes biblically-accurate books for adults and children.

If you are looking for quality Bible teaching for children then we have a wide and excellent range of Bible story books - from board books to teenage fiction, we have it covered.

You can also try our new Bible teaching Syllabus for 3-9 year olds and teaching materials for pre-school children.

These children's books are bright, fun and full of biblical truth, an ideal way to help children discover Jesus Christ for themselves. Our aim is to help children find out about God and get them enthusiastic about reading the Bible, now and later in their lives.

Find us at our web page:
www.christianfocus.com